I Walked My Dog This Morning

ISBN **978-1-935786-76-4**

Printed in the United States of America

St. Clair Publications
P. O. Box 726
Mc Minnville, TN 37111—0726

http://stclairpublications.com

Cover Design

Stanley J. St. Clair

Front Cover Photo

Rhonda St. Clair

I Walked My Dog This Morning

and other poems of the 21st Century

by

Stanley J. St. Clair

CONTENTS

DEDICATION

This collection of all new poetical verse is dedicated to the memory of my special son, Scott, and my special cat, Fonzie. How does one compare a man and a cat? Really, one cannot. But, there are some common threads. I made a decision to adopt both of them at an early age. Both of their lives were cut short tragically during the last half of 2014. They both had traits which sometimes worried me, but most importantly, I had a strong and special love for them both.

I pray that God in his mercy will allow them to again flood my being in the next life.

I WALKED MY DOG THIS MORNING

I took my dog for a walk this morning

'Ere the advent of the sun.

Fall was heavy in the air

And the first hint of frost lay low on the lawn.

A lazy three-quarter moon

Hung tight against a treetop in the West.

Could this truly be the same shy moon

Which hid behind earth's black shadow

Two mere nights ago?

My doggie paused to smell and mark his territory

Then pulled forcefully ahead.

By dawn's encroaching glimmer

The ruddy and blanching leaves

Dotted the darkened greens about me

As onward we ambled around our suburban block.

A brown fringe of fallen foliage

Lined the edge of asphalt.

My small companion stopped and sniffed

7

Where yesterday had laid a silenced squirrel,

Its relative barking incessantly

From the quivering limbs above.

Some kind soul had scooped it up

And whisked it away from the view of passersby.

As we rounded the corner, morn's soft rays

Arose in the East as a florescent vapor.

The roar of the mowers had been quelled for the season,

I mused, and I was glad.

We soon were home again—safe and warm.

10-21-13 - In honor of Lee Pennington, Former Kentucky Poet Laureate and personal friend

OUR RENDEZVOUS WITH THE MOON

We didn't soar in a rocket ship

On our rendezvous with the moon,

We simply took a leisurely stroll

'Neath its silvery light as May gave way to June.

While entranced on a bench by a willow tree

I crooned a new love tune;

And memories were sealed for aye,

On our rendezvous with the moon.

10-27-13

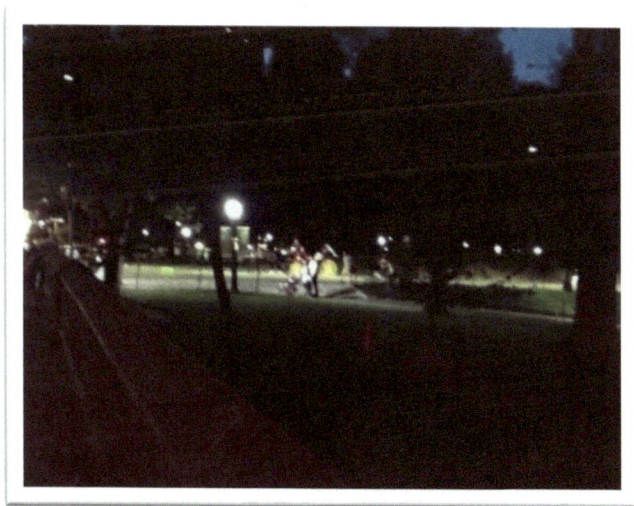

Night in Central Park, NYC (Photo Stan St. Clair)

UNPREPARED

He cocked his head to seize my glance,

So unprepared for circumstance;

A blackish ring encircled his eye

Like a Spuds McKinsey tattoo gone awry.

12-13-13

NATURE SPEAKS

As I gazed out this morning

Ma Nature's voice was plain;

The red sky spoke of marching clouds

And close impending rain.

1-9-14

Red Morning in Mountain Green (Photo Stan St. Clair)

EARLY APRIL'S PLAY

I wipe the frost from Time's great book

And slowly turn a warmer page.

There lovely April's graceful form

Begins to set the welcomed stage.

From Bradford Pears white petals puff

Upon the wings of April's breeze.

Not long ago this ground was gripped

In dreadful Winter's staggering freeze.

11

The lea bursts forth in blushing blossom;

Bees collect their nectar fair.

The robin's song reminds the chipmunk

Mating season fills the air.

Bulbous tulips shyly peek

Out from their robes of brilliant green.

Forsythias and dogwoods smile

As Spring walks forth upon the scene.

4-12-14

Early April at Home (Photo Stan St. Clair)

WHY DO DOGS EAT GRASS?

Another man who walks his dog

Stopped me and mine today.

"Does yours eat grass?" my neighbor asked;

"He does," I had to say.

I don't know why they do it though,

Is something there they lack?

Doggies pause and munch awhile,

Like we would grab a snack.

4-15, 17-14

CRAZY WEATHER

It's Passover.

Upon its eve three were slain by the hand of a neo-Nazi.

The blood moon came,

The blood moon went;

It hid behind the clouds.

It must be 'Dogwood Winter';

It's snowing on the blossoms.

13

The dog went out but didn't like it.

The day wares on;

The cold wind swirls.

Tomorrow morning frost shall greet us.

The garden may cry, "Uncle!"

4-15-14

DANDELIONS

The dainty dandelions dot the lawns

And stretch their silvery seeds toward the heavens.

Since no angelic hand awaits to retrieve them

A faint puffy breeze releases their hoary offering,

Presenting it back to Mother Earth with genial glee.

The soft raindrops pepper them downward

Exhibiting obvious pride in a mission accomplished.
4-23, 24-14

THE MAIN ATTRACTION

Various sights and sundry sounds

Attract my dog as we circle the block.

The gruff and guttural growl

Of a huge bulldog

Causes him to whine

And pull in its direction.

The pavement's still moist

From the overnight rain,

So he eases into the grass —

He has spied his main attraction.

This one is yellow and green, not red;

But he doesn't mind.

It's a fire hydrant and he's a male dog.

4-29-14

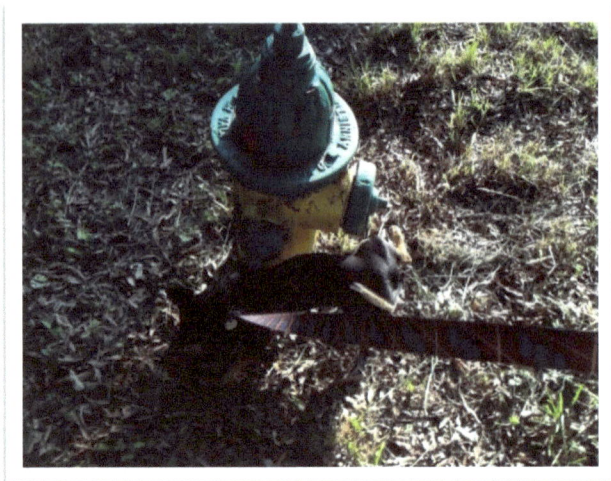

The Main Attraction (Photo Stan St. Clair)

THROUGH TINY CANINE EYES

Just set your spirit free

For a brief and fleeting span.

Come dwell within my little furry form.

It's amazing what one might see

Through the eyes of a confident canine.

I raise my feet ever so high beside the road

As the mammoth blades of green strike my jowls.

I sniff the base of a tree—

16

Another male has preceded me!

I lift my leg and replace his scent with mine.

My human pulls my restraining cord.

He wants to keep me mobile.

A fluffy creature, smaller that I,

Darts across the way, barely at my front!

I lunge toward it to beg it to play.

It zips through a yard

And up the slender trunk of a sapling.

My human speaks kind tones

And continues his march toward home.

He is so big and I am but a tiny creature;

At least that is what most must think.

But in my mind I fear no one and all is fighting fit.

5-4-14

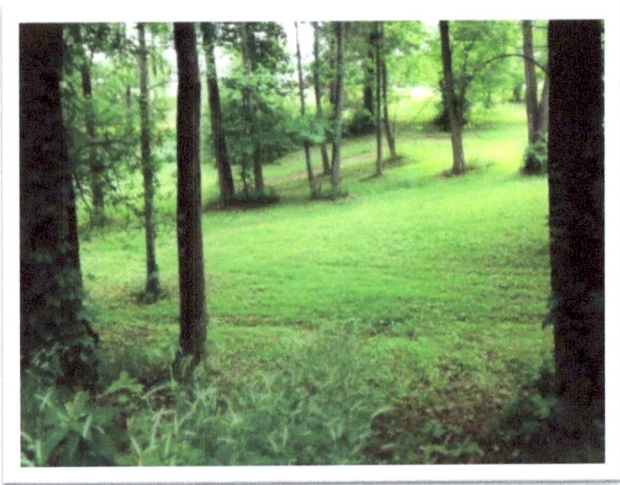

The Park

THE PARK

The woods in the park, hard by our house,

Is full of furry game.

When a hare spots my dog, it dashes right out,

Then a squirrel in a tree does the same.

A female Jay sails down as to say,

"Don't upset our applecart!

T'is our home, don't you see, so just let us be!"

Methinks that the bird may be smart.

5-1-14

DEER? OH, DEAR!

This morning strolling up a lane,

The dog leash in my hand,

There at a yonder distance

I judge a doe did stand.

I squinted oh so warily

To verify my sight,

When off the creature bounded

In the subtle breaking light.

And then it was, I realized

The visitor was canine —

A large one though, he'd been,

Disguised by mist and pine.

6-21-14

HOPE

It's not the best and not the worst

But wavering in between.

Crayola candles blue and yellow

Melting into green.

The wick is flickering in a lamp;

A beam drifts through the fog.

Then plunging onward into darkness

Daggers pierce the bog.

Soft raindrops splash into a keg

Beneath a mangled oak

Then bravely peeping through a cloud

Faint light the fetters broke.

8-9-14

In loving memory of Scott

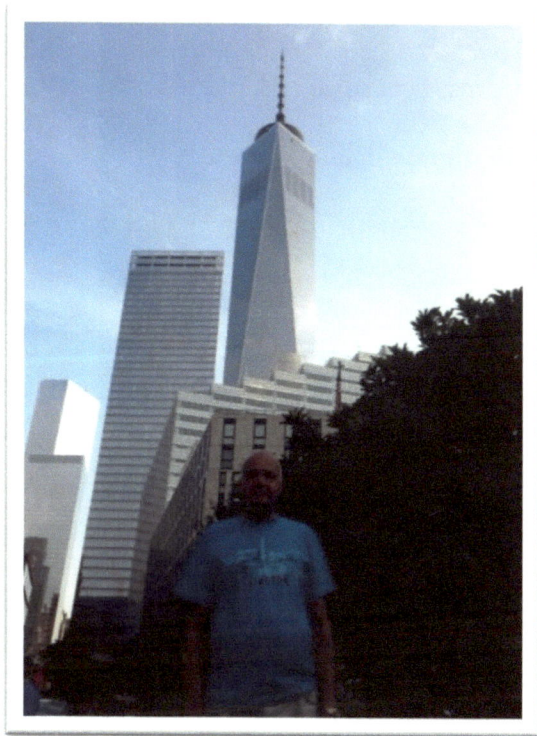

At Ground Zero (Photo Steve St. Clair)

I'VE BEEN THERE

I've trampled old bricks; the Forbidden City

And ambled up China's Great Wall.

I've forged to the summit of grim Kilauea

And basked in the mist; Yelapa's quaint fall.

21

I've roamed the mystical ruins of Mayans;

And dined with dignity; Halifax coast.

I've pounded the pavement in Lower Manhattan,

But mused at Ground Zero the most.

I've savored the chicory at Café du Monde

And ogled the dives on Bourbon Street;

I've chauffeured a coupe through Charlotte Amalie,

And trudged endless miles of soft golden wheat.

I met Jimmy Carter and Jimmy Doolittle,

Made friends with both nobles and peasants.

The rays of the sun have fallen around me

Upon the great shrines and the deserts.

The White House before me, the West to my right,

I've lifted my heart in great praise,

Remembering Old Faithful blubbering heavenward,

My love for creation ablaze.

9-10-14; Remembering 9-11

Dedicated to Steve St. Clair

FOREVER AND A DAY

Once again the air is crisp

When I walk my dog in the mornings.

Evening shadows faster fall

On Mountain Green these days.

Clocking out as our protector

Our brave li'l' boy lies down to rest

Before his summer hour.

Two huge canines have fast approached

While we were walking Brody,

But he was not afraid a bit

Though they have threatened fiercely.

We love him like the other members

Of our closest family,

And hope that he remains with us

Forever and a day.

9-24-14

Our Protector (Photo Stan St. Clair)

Fonzie at Rest (Photo Stan St. Clair)

OUR CAT GOT OUT

Our cat got out again last night,

That callous, stubborn feline!

Sometimes he spies an open door

And for it makes a bee-line.

We tried and tried to coax him in

But he played cat and mouse.

O'er night he chose the out-of-doors

Above the comforts of the house.

25

This morning at the door he stood

And darted in with glee.

I can't figure Fonzie out—

Not for the life of me.

9-26-14

THE FOCUS OF OUR LENS

I know that I cannot return to the past,

For it is but an elusive trail

Of botched memories:

A crape paper kite floating ever upward;

Its gingham tail with knotted bows

Flapping behind in the misty breeze

Of wanton dreams.

No, the past, as the future,

Is hardly as the camera of the mind envisions.

Both are best unaltered;

Accepted just as they are.

26

We live in the uniqueness of the moment,

And that must be the focus of our lens.

10-9-14

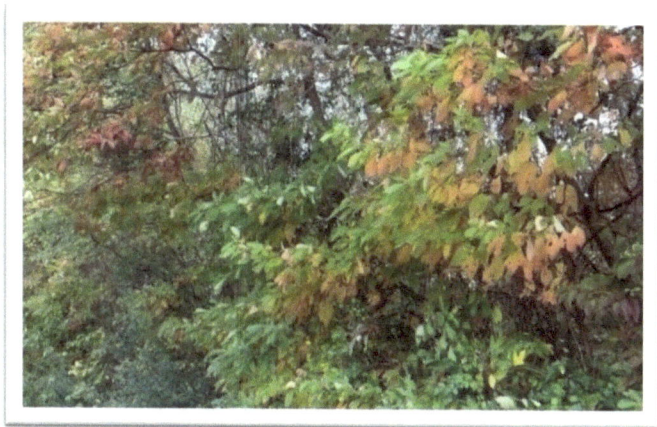

Mottled Hues of Autumn (Photo Stan St. Clair)

CHANGES

My digits firmly grip the leash

As Brody drags me westward.

Mottled hues of autumn

Now greet my glassy gaze.

27

My focused mind ignores them;

For this day's chosen actions

Will forever alter life.

10-10-14

LIFE AND SEASONS

Halloween approaches fast.

Sir Autumn has donned

His dazzling kilt—

His yellow mustache

Waves from the willow.

His balding cranium

Relinquishes its deadened tresses.

Soon a pallid blanket

Will envelop all that endures.

Fluffy clouds of mutation

Drift through the boughs.

While one is departing,

Another arrives,

28

Life and seasons

Nourish change.

10-29-14

HALLOWEEN MARCH

Gremlins, goblins, ghosts and ghouls,

Amble onward — they're no fools!

Alex Chandon, Dante, Poe

Bear the torch, as on they go;

Glossy-eyed, they play their game,

Making mock and taunting shame.

Oh, here they are, at my front door!

"Trick or treat!" I hear them roar.

10-30-14

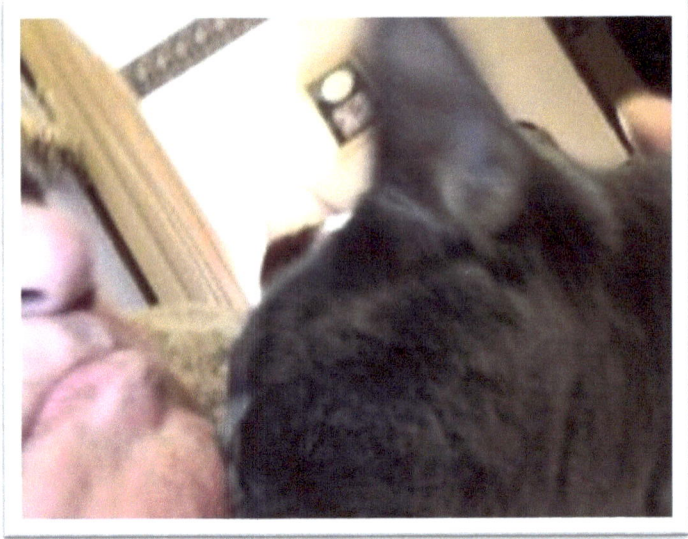

A painful memory

FROSTY MORNING

It was a frosty morning in mid-December

As I walked my dog once more.

I blankly stared through the fine bare limbs

Of a giant maple at a dark gazebo.

The silver-grey skies beyond

Reminded me of the gloomy focus

Of my troubled soul.

30

The five past days were filled with angst.

Our rambling cat had dashed away

As we were leaving home at night.

Because before he'd been there waiting

At the door the following morning,

That is what we thought would be.

But not this time.

Every effort I made to find him

Proved another fruitless gesture.

Then yesterday I told a neighbor

To keep a watch for him.

An hour later she came calling.

Out on the highway near her house,

Our cat had been struck down.

I brought him home; laid him to rest

Beside two other loved ones.

Every second December,

We've lost a pet;

Our hearts have been distressed.

Rest in peace, our Fonzie, dear,

You're gone, but never far.

12-13-14

IT

An animal is not an "it,"

But properly, a he or she.

Tell me now, how would you feel

If "it" were you or me?

1-3-15

A PROVERB

Which is more to be desired,

A rod of iron, or peace of mind?

Brute force is flaunted by the youth

But Wisdom is garnered by sculpted maturity.

3-4-15

The Thinker (Photo Public Domain)

LOVE TO LOVE

The morning grass was more intense

Sporting crystal droplets

As glimmering rays slipped through

The shifting sky.

Brody urged me in the door,

Begging for his bacon treat.

33

An hour after,

There was Charlie

Strolling with his Benji

Through the vacant tennis court:

The score was love to love.

3-26-2015

JUST SAYIN'

A robin redbreast isn't really red — it's orange!

The black box on a plane is orange too.

I suppose that poets bent on endless rhyme

Will soon be calling oranges tangerine…

Just sayin'

3-30-15

HEAVENWARD

Hemlocks and hollies

And ponderous pines

Hang out through the winter

With ice in their tines;

Now poplars and pears,

Their blooms so divine

Climb out from seclusion

To greet heaven's shine.

A new day is dawning

In our hemisphere

And prayers for a future

Not riddled with fear.

4-3-15

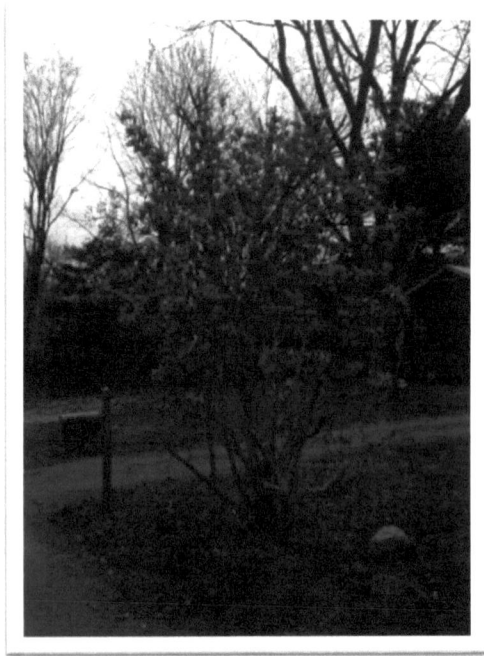

Blooms so Divine

THE VOICE WITHIN

Deep within the heart of man

There rests a still small voice.

It breathes out whispers to the mind

In favor of the prudent choice.

Sometimes we heed and grasp a Truth,

At other times it's brushed away.

Conscience, Higher Self or God,

There is no doubt it's there to stay.

4-22-15

ABOUT THE POET

Stanley J. "Stan" St.Clair is the founder and owner of **St.Clair Publications** in McMinnville, TN, found online at http://stclairpublications.com, and a retired insurance agent/manager. In addition to a designation of LUTCF from the National Association of Life Underwriters in Washington, DC, he has a degree in Religious Education from Covington College and Theological Seminary. Stan's articles, poetry, and numerous books have been published around the world in at least four countries. He was featured in the 2007-2008 *Cambridge Who's Who, Honors Edition*, and the *International Who's Who in Poetry* in 2004. He has traveled extensively around the globe, has met a number of dignitaries and counts well-known authors among his friends.

Stan's first collection of poetry, *Reflections on Life* contained numerous entries which had previously been published in newspapers, magazines and books. This color-illustrated volume is all new verse written in the past two years. His best-selling tome, *Most Comprehensive Origins of Clichés, Proverbs and Figurative Expressions* has been well received in several countries, and has ranked in the top one percent of all paperbacks on Amazon for the past two years.

Stan is married to the former Rhonda Prater, is a member and former elder of the Cumberland Presbyterian Church; a charter member who has served in all offices of the Warren County Kiwanis Club and past Lt. Governor of the KY-TN District of Kiwanis International; a member of the Highland Rim Scottish Society, a Commissioner and former Eastern Vice President of

Clan Sinclair, USA, and co-founder of St. Clair Research and its worldwide DNA Project found online at stclairresearch.com.

www.ingramcontent.com/pod-product-compliance
Lightning Source LLC
Chambersburg PA
CBHW040346060426
42445CB00029B/15